ETHICAL
DEBATES

Stem Cell
Research

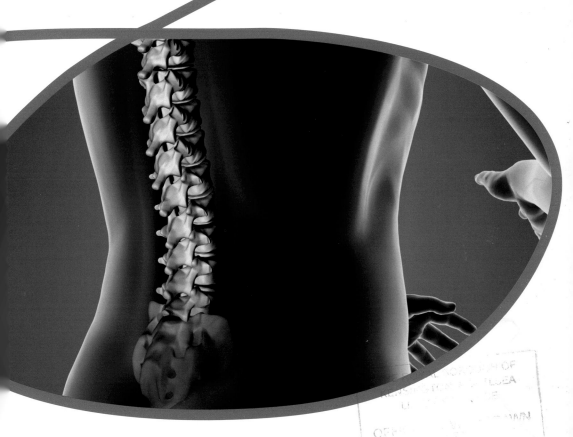

PETE MOORE

Published in 2013 by Wayland
Copyright © 2013 Wayland

Wayland
338 Euston Road
London NW1 3BH

Wayland Australia
Level 17/207 Kent Street
Sydney NSW 2000

Editor: Katie Woolley
Designer: Rita Storey

British Library Cataloguing in Publication
data

Moore, Pete, 1962-
   Stem-cell research. -- (Ethical debates)
   1. Stem cells--Research--Moral and
   ethical aspects--
   Juvenile literature.
   I. Title II. Series
   174.2'8-dc22

ISBN: 978 0 7502 8205 5

Printed in China

10 9 8 7 6 5 4 3 2 1

Wayland is a division of Hachette
Children's Books,
an Hachette UK company.
www.hachette.co.uk

Acknowledgements:
Mads Abildgaard/istockphoto: 1, 12.
AFP/Getty Images: 27.ancroft/Shutterstock:
19. AP/PA: 31. Joel Blit/istockphoto: 15.
Bloomberg/Getty Images: 37. Eric
Delmar/istockphoto: 23.Eugin.net: 13.
Evaristo SA/AFP/Getty Images: 5b.
© Copyright 2001, Georgia Institute of
Technology: 9b. Getty Images: 29.
Jose Gil/Shutterstock: 33. Steve
Greer/istockphoto: 34.
haak78/Shutterstock: 22. Jubal
Harshaw/Shutterstock: 8. Patrick
Hertzog/AFP/Getty Images: 38. Jeremy
Sutton Hibbert/Rex Features: 21.
Imagebroker /Alamy: front cover, 44.
Insight-Visual UK/Rex Features: 10.
Lebrecht Music & Arts/Alamy: 18.
Lee Jin Man/AP/PAI: 41. Dr G Moscoso/SPL:
9t. R.Nagy/Shutterstock: 20. National
Cancer Institute/SPL: 32. Nature Publishing
group: 17. Ng Huan Gon/AP/PAI: 40.
Photos12/Alamy: 28. Spencer Platt/Getty
Images: 42. Bill Pugliano/Getty Images: 35.
Stephanie Schaerer: 42. Steve G
Schmeissner/SPL: 16. Tim Sloan/AFP/Getty
Features: 11. SPL: 30. Jason
Steel/Shutterstock: 14. Justin
Sullivan/Getty Images: 5t. Tanuki
Photography/istockphoto: 24. Shawn
Thew/Getty Images: 36. vipflash
/Shutterstock: 25. wikimedia. C.C.: 26.
Dr Nikos Yorgas /SPL: 6. Nikos Yogas
/Wellcome Images: 45.

Every attempt has been made to clear
copyright. Should there be any
inadvertent omission please apply to the
publisher for rectification.

About the Consultant: Dr Patricia Macnair
is a hospital physician working in a small
rehabilitation hospital with elderly patients
who are recovering from major illness. She
has a Masters degree in Medical Ethics and
Medical Law.

contents

Real-life case study

This real-life case study highlights some of the issues that surround the debate on stem cell research.

case study

Spinal repair

On 11 October 2010 Geron Corporation, a biotechnology company based in the US, announced a new development in the science of stem cells. They had just treated the first patient using a newly developed treatment. Scientists had taken cells from human embryos that had been growing for less than a week and had carefully controlled the way that these cells grew in laboratory conditions. They had then injected these cells into the spine of a patient whose spinal cord had recently been damaged in an accident. The cells they injected are called stem cells.

The spinal cord is the complex bundle of nerve fibres that runs through our vertebrae. Acting like a massive telephone cable, it carries information from the brain to our body, and signals from our body back to our brain. Around 12,000 people in the US alone have accidents each year in which the nerves in the bundle of nerve fibres in their spines are damaged and this bundle can no longer carry nerve messages.

The doctors hope that by injecting stem cells into the area of injury, they will be able to repair the damaged spinal cord. If all goes well, these stem cells will wrap around the damaged nerve fibres, and help them to work again.

Not everyone is excited about the possibilities of stem cell research. Many people are worried that the scientists and doctors at Geron Corporation had obtained the stem cells by first creating and then destroying human embryos. They argue that human embryos are fully human, and say that vulnerable lives were taken to create this therapy. Others worry that the cells may get out of control and keep growing. If they do this, the cells may create a cancerous tumour that could do even more damage to the patient's spinal cord.

A further anxiety is that any patient involved in these early trials is taking quite a risk with their life. Others worry that we are spending vast amounts of money developing treatments that save only a few people, while millions of people die each year from diseases that we already know how to prevent if only there was enough money.

viewpoints

'Initiating [this trial] is a milestone for the field of human embryonic stem cell-based therapies.'
Dr Thomas B. Okarma, president and CEO of Geron, 2010

'Even many pro-embryonic stem cell scientists have expressed concerns about Geron's trial, that it is not proven even in rats. The concern for many of us is that Geron is endangering patients' health and very lives, to make a political point and increase their stock price.'
Dr David Prentice, a former professor at Indiana State University, www.lifenews.com, 2010

▲ Senator Barbara Boxer (left), looks at stem cells, as seen through a microscope, on a television monitor during a laboratory tour at Geron Corporation in July 2003. Senator Boxer promised employees at Geron Corporation to fight for support for their stem cell research.

▼ There are people who argue that supporting the use of human embryos in stem cell research is ethically unacceptable. Below, protestors stand outside the Brazilian Supreme Court in 2008, on the day the Court will decide if stem cell research can take place in Brazil with certain restrictions.

CHAPTER 1

What are stem cells?

All living organisms are made of tiny cells. We are made of billions of them. Look at your finger. Take out a ruler and measure a line two centimetres (cm) in length. That two centimetre line goes over something like 1,000 cells. Each of these microscopic cells is packed with the biological machinery needed to keep it alive, and to perform specific tasks. Each cell in the body contains a nucleus. This nucleus is like a library of information, all stored on a two millimetre (mm) long, threadlike molecule of DNA. It is this biological library that contains all of the information needed to build a human being and can be found in almost every cell in the body.

From the beginning

Every human being started out as just one information-laden cell – a fertilized egg. This one cell grew, and then split into two identical cells. A few hours later those two cells divided into four, and the four into eight, 16, 32, 64. All of this happened

▼ Hundreds of sperm reach an egg but only one will break in and fertilize it. Stem cells develop from a single fertilized egg.

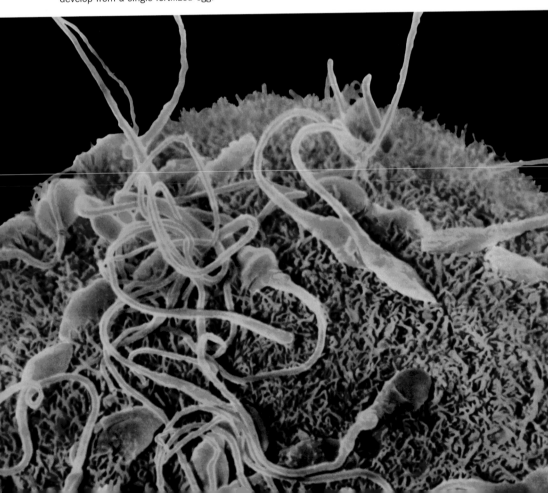

while the little bundle of cells, called the morula, was travelling down the mother's fallopian tube, a thin tube that connects the egg-producing ovaries to the uterus (or womb).

Around four to six days after fertilization the cells form a hollow ball with a clump of cells inside. Scientists call this a blastocyst. The outer sphere of cells is called the trophoblast and this develops into the placenta, which feeds the embryo during pregnancy. The inner cell mass grows into the embryo itself.

When stem cells specialise

At this stage of development, all of the cells in the inner cell mass of the blastocyst are stem cells. This means they have the potential to develop into any tissue type in the body, such as bone, liver, nerves or blood. Over the following weeks as these cells grow and divide, they gradually become increasingly specialised.

Most of these cells will go on to develop and form parts of a specific organ. When this happens they no longer have the potential to change, divide or multiply. However, some cells retain their ability to divide. For example, there are stem cells in the skin that generate new skin cells if you cut or graze yourself. These are often called adult stem cells because they are the type of stem cell found in adults. Scientists call them somatic stem cells. It is these stem cells that are active when we are growing, and that step in to repair damage when necessary.

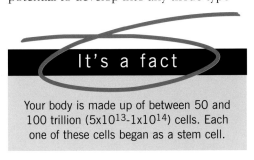

It's a fact

Your body is made up of between 50 and 100 trillion ($5 \times 10^{13} - 1 \times 10^{14}$) cells. Each one of these cells began as a stem cell.

▼ This diagram below shows the stages of development from fertilization to the early embryo. During the embryo's development, its stem cells also develop and change.

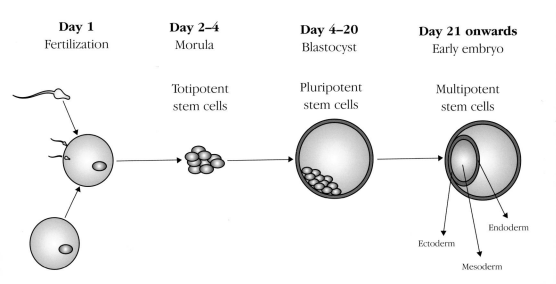

Day 1	Day 2–4	Day 4–20	Day 21 onwards
Fertilization	Morula	Blastocyst	Early embryo
	Totipotent stem cells	Pluripotent stem cells	Multipotent stem cells

Ectoderm

Endoderm

Mesoderm

Differences in stem cells

Not all stem cells have the same capabilities. What they can do varies depending on where you find them. Many scientists who are involved in stem cell research believe that it is more exciting to study the ones that can form many different types of tissue than the ones that have more specific functions.

Totipotent cells

When a sperm joins with an egg at fertilization, the cell that is formed rapidly starts to grow and divide. Within two to four days, it will have become a small bundle of around 100 cells called the morula. These cells are remarkably powerful. Scientists can divide them into small clusters and watch each develop into genetically identical embryos. Each one is healthy, and each one is fully intact. It is basically what happens with identical twins, where an embryo splits in two and each half then develops into a complete baby. Because these cells can develop into any type of tissue in the body, scientists call them 'totipotent'.

Becoming more restricted

By the second week after fertilization, the cells have formed a blastocyst, a hollow ball, with a mass of cells inside. From this point on each cell starts to take on characteristics of one particular tissue type, and as this occurs the stem cells that are left become much more restricted. At first they are called 'pluripotent'. This means that they have the potential to develop into many types of tissue, and then 'multipotent' indicating that they can generate into only a few. Some become specialised tissue stem cells that can only form one type of cell.

case study

First totipotent experiments

As long ago as the 1890s, German biologist Hans Driesch performed many experiments on sea urchin embryos. In one, he shook a two-celled embryo in a beaker full of sea water until the two cells separated. Over the following weeks, each cell grew independently, and formed a separate, whole sea urchin.

In 1902 another German embryologist, Hans Spemann, repeated the idea by taking a fertilized salamander egg and waited for it to grow into two cells, then separated the cells. Each of the cells developed into identical adult salamanders.

In each case, scientists proved that the cells in the early embryos were totipotent. This early scientific research laid the foundations for stem cell research.

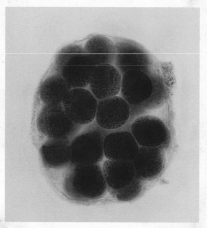

▲ Studying sea urchin embryos gave important insights into stem cell science.

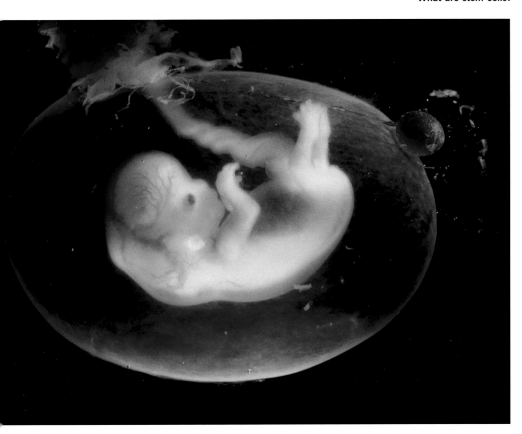

▲ This is an eight-week-old human embryo. By this stage of the embryo's development, most of its cells have become specialised and are no longer totipotent stem cells, however a few retain their flexibility and can still be used in stem cell research.

It's a fact

The ectoderm, mesoderm and endoderm are different layers of cells within the developing early embryo. Each layer of stem cells has the ability to grow into certain types of tissue and organs.

Ectoderm	Mesoderm	Endoderm
skin	blood cells	gut lining
brain	blood vessels	lungs
eyes	skeleton	liver
nervous system	muscle	pancreas

Why the excitement?

Most of the world's medical effort is aimed at helping people to grow healthily and repair damage caused by illness, accident or ageing. In our bodies, stem cells work to do just that. Stem cells exist in the embryo as cells so it can grow and develop, and in later life somatic stem cells step in to repair damage.

Many scientists are keen to understand how stem cells help the body keep itself in good condition, as well as discovering what goes wrong in many different diseases. In addition, if they can find out how stem cells work, how to create them and how to control them, they will be able to develop new treatments. For example, they might boost the body's natural ability to keep itself healthy by deliberately adding extra health-restoring stem cells.

Supporters of stem cell research argue that stem cells can also be very useful in laboratory research. Once a population of these cells is growing in a laboratory, they will continue to grow and divide forever, providing an endless supply of identical cells. Instead of using laboratory animals to test experimental drugs, scientists can use these cells. This is particularly effective when they want to look at thousands of slightly different chemicals to see if any have useful properties, for example as medicine. Scientists can quickly and cheaply expose a few hundred cells to each chemical, when it would be impractical and unethical to do the same with tens of thousands of animals.

Why the controversy?

The key issue is that the stem cells that excite many scientists are often taken from embryos, and to obtain these

◄ On 5 March, 2002 Christopher Reeve, the actor who played Superman before he was paralysed in 1995, campaigned for embryonic stem cell research at a US Senate hearing.

v i e w p o i n t s

'Recent published reports on the isolation and successful culturing of the first human pluripotent stem cell lines have generated great excitement and have brought biomedical research to the edge of a new frontier.'
National Institutes of Health, USA, 2000

'Embryonic stem cell research is at the leading edge of a series of moral hazards.'
President George W. Bush, 9 August 2001

▲ In July 2006, the then US President, George W. Bush announced his veto of the US stem cell research bill to an audience that included children born from frozen embryos. This veto banned the public funding of embryonic stem cell research. President Bush said the bill 'would support the taking of innocent life.'

human stem cells scientists need to use human embryos during their research. When the cells are removed from the embryo, the embryo is then destroyed. The destruction of the embryo is the major ethical issue surrounding stem cell research.

As we will see throughout this book, people have widely differing views about whether an embryo is a full human being or a ball of cells yet to become a 'life', but most people believe that human embryos should be treated with respect. The question is whether using them in scientific research and medical therapies is ethically acceptable.

Furthermore, people are also concerned about the ethics of the risks that are taken by the first patients who are given these cells during treatment, as well as the way that companies make profits from scientific and medical discoveries that use, and destroy, human embryos.

summary

▶ The cells in the morula can form any type of tissue in the body – these cells are called totipotent.

▶ Stem cells from the blastocyst stage (forms four to six days after fertilization) can make many different types of tissues in the body – these cells are pluripotent.

▶ Stem cells taken from a foetus more than nine weeks old, a baby or an adult can only develop into a few types of tissues – they are called multipotent.

▶ Many people believe it is not ethical to collect stem cells from embryos which must then be destroyed.

CHAPTER 2

Sources of stem cells

As we have seen, one of the best places to find stem cells is in the morula and blastocyst stages of human embryonic development (see page 7). At this stage all the stem cells are capable of becoming many types of tissue in our body. As such, these cells are naturally extremely versatile and there are various ways that scientists can obtain them.

Stem cells from in vitro fertilization

One way of obtaining stem cells is through in vitro fertilization (IVF). Around one in six couples have difficulty conceiving when they try to have a baby. For a wide variety of reasons the woman cannot get pregnant. Some couples solve this by using IVF. With in vitro fertilization, doctors collect up to a dozen eggs from the woman and the man supplies a sperm sample. Laboratory technicians then bring the eggs and sperm together and, if the procedure is successful, the couple will end up with six or seven embryos. Two of these embryos are then placed in the woman's womb and this may lead to her becoming pregnant and having a child. In the UK, regulators ask doctors to use a maximum of two embryos at a time – using more runs the risk of having triplets. Having three babies at once can lead to the foetuses growing poorly and being born prematurely, both of which may be harmful for the babies and the mother.

The couple is then left with spare embryos. These can either be destroyed, or frozen so that the couple can use them to have more children in the future, or if the first attempt at IVF fails and the parents want to try again. There is one more option. Couples can give these embryos to scientists to be used as sources of stem cells.

This is highly controversial. Some people say that this is a good use of 'spare' embryos. They argue that these small bundles of human cells should be used to create therapies that can heal conditions in children and adults. Other people say that the human embryo is still a life and so

▼ The use of stem cells in laboratory conditions is highly controversial. While stem cell research could potentially lead to the successful treatment of people with life-threatening illness or physical disability, such as those suffering from spinal injuries, its critics argue that the research places little value on the rights of the embryo.

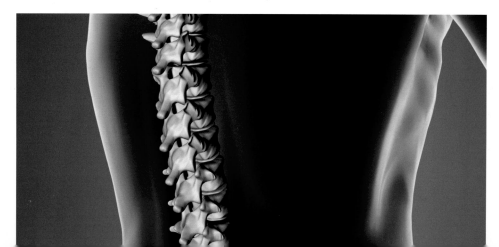

▲ There are now websites, like this one, where it is possible to buy and sell human eggs on the Internet. These eggs could be used in stem cell research. However, some opponents of stem cell research say this is ethically unacceptable.

should have the same rights as a human being and, as such, should not be harmed in any way. Still others, for example the Roman Catholic Church, believe that the process of IVF is unethical and that an egg and sperm should only come together inside a woman's body. It is wrong for technology and science to interfere in the creation of a new human being.

Stem cells created specially

As scientists develop more ways of using stem cells, many argue that they will never get enough stem cells if they are only allowed to use surplus embryos. One solution would be to deliberately fertilize eggs and create embryos for the sole purpose of harvesting stem cells, but this does raise more ethical issues.

It's a fact

In June 2009, New York State became the first US state to let scientists use public money to buy eggs from women. These eggs can be used to create embryos for research.

viewpoints

'We pay people to participate in research that has zero benefit to them [but carries] risk all the time, and we trust people to make that decision for themselves.'
Debra Mathews, Johns Hopkins Berman Institute of Bioethics, *Scientific American,* 17 November 2009

'There are devastating reports, especially in the US where this is common, of egg donors losing their own fertility or even dying during the procedure.'
Josephine Quintavalle, director of Comment on Reproductive Ethics (CORE)

Parthenogenesis

There may be another option for scientists. Normally human eggs grow into embryos after joining with a sperm. In some animals, however, eggs can start to grow on their own and go on to produce offspring. This process is called parthenogenesis, but it never normally happens in mammals. In June 2007, International Stem Cell Corporation, a California-based stem cell research company, claimed that they had intentionally created human stem cells from unfertilized human eggs by triggering parthenogenesis.

These cells came from an unfertilized egg, so they could not have developed into a full human being. Consequently some people may believe that they are not embryos. As such, using these stem cells could possibly get around the ethical problems of using embryos for stem cell research, but the process is not risk free. The very fact that these cells do not develop normally highlights that they are not totally normal cells, so scientists question whether it is safe to inject them into a human being.

Aborted foetuses

It is also possible to source stem cells from aborted foetuses. While the most versatile stem cells come from the morula and blastocyst, you can still find very useful stem cells later in foetal development. Once an embryo has grown for eight weeks it has developed all of its basic organs, even though it is roughly only three centimetres long. From now until adulthood, the organs of the foetus grow in size and develop their ability to function. Consequently, from the eighth week of development onwards, most cells have become dedicated to performing a specific task.

However, a few pockets of stem cells remain that can rebuild specific tissues. Rather than being the pluripotent, or even totipotent stem cells seen in earlier

▼ Many lizards produce eggs that can grow into new offspring through parthenogenesis, even if they are not fertilized. Now scientists are finding ways of stimulating human eggs, so they can start to develop into an embryo even though they have not been fertilized by a sperm. These embryos could then be used in stem cell research.

embryos, these stem cells are called multipotent because they can generate a limited range of cells. Scientists can obtain these cells by carefully extracting the stem cells from aborted human foetuses, isolating the cells and growing them in laboratory conditions.

Some people suggest that using aborted foetuses to supply stem cells for research or therapy reduces the ethical issues raised by abortion because embryonic stem cells that would otherwise have been destroyed are not wasted.

Umbilical cord blood and adults

When a baby is growing in a mother's womb, all the nutrients and oxygen that it needs travel from the placenta through a set of blood vessels in the umbilical cord. Once the baby has been born, this cord is normally thrown away, along with the placenta. Blood can be collected from the umbilical cord and the placenta and used as a source of pluripotent stem cells. Gathering the stem cells is ethically unproblematic because the process does not harm any individual and no human embryos are used or destroyed in the process. However, the pluripotent stem cells removed in this process are not as versatile as the totipotent stem cells that are found in the morula stage of human embryonic development. So while this process is ethically preferable, stem cell research scientists still require stem cells harvested from human embryos.

It is also possible to take tissue samples from adults and use sophisticated laboratory techniques to turn them into stem cells. One way is to take a human egg and remove almost all of the genetic information that it is carrying. At the same time scientists take a piece of tissue from an adult, and separate it into individual cells. The 'empty' egg is then placed next to one of the adult cells. In the right conditions, the two combine and start to grow into an embryo. The cells that grow are genetically identical to the adult who gave the initial tissue sample. Some people approve of this cloning process because the cells will perfectly match the original donor. Others say that it is ethically wrong because the process still involves creating and wasting an embryo (a new life).

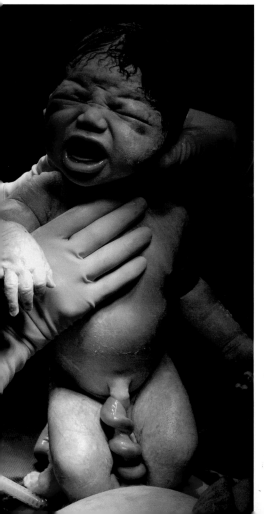

◄ Making use of the blood collected from the umbilical cord and the placenta of new born babies is a way of harvesting stem cells without using and destroying human embryos.

Induced pluripotent stem cells

Since 2006, scientists have been able to take specialised cells from adult tissue and 'reprogramme' them so that they become pluripotent (see page 8), meaning the cells are capable of developing into many types of tissue. This is a particularly exciting development for people who are worried that it is unethical to use human embryos. Cells produced this way are called induced pluripotent stem cells, a term that is normally abbreviated to iPS cells. The first experiments were done using cells taken from mice, but soon scientists worked out how to create iPS cells from a tissue sample donated by a human donor.

A key advantage of this process is that the iPS cells are genetically identical to the cells in the original donor. This means that the iPS cells could more easily be put back into the donor to treat diseases or repair damage, because the body is less likely to reject them. iPS cells could also be used to test experimental drugs, study whether chemicals are toxic to humans and create experimental models that let scientists study different diseases.

▼ This coloured scanning electron micrograph shows an embryonic stem cell sitting in the eye of a needle. Stem cells created through iPS could remove the ethical problems raised by the previous need to destroy embryos to carry out stem cell research.

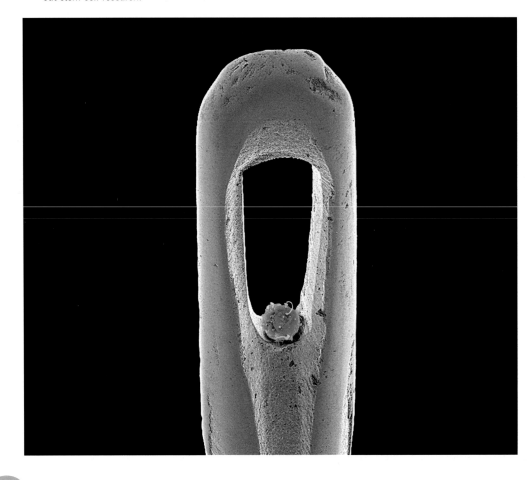

case study

Pluripotent stem cell research

A team of researchers from Boston University's Center for Regenerative Medicine and the Pulmonary Center have generated 100 new types of human-induced pluripotent stem cell. Each type of cell started from tissue donated by individuals who had various lung diseases, including cystic fibrosis and emphysema. The scientists want to use these cells to study new treatments for a range of debilitating diseases.

The scientists who created these cells are excited by the fact that they did not need to use human embryonic cells for this work, and believe that these induced cells are easier to obtain than cells from human embryos.

To harvest the cells the scientists took skin samples from adults who had a recognised lung disease. The scientists then grew the cells in a laboratory, examined them and tested different drugs on them to potentially find cures for these lung diseases.

▲ The internationally renowned scientific journal *Nature Biotechnology* is often the place where scientists publish important findings. Research findings about induced pluripotent stem cells were published in this edition in January 2008.

The risks involved

However, as with much scientific research there are risks involved which must be considered. To induce the donated cells, scientists have to insert three or four extra genes. These genes stimulate the cell to start growing, but there is a risk that once the cells have been inserted into a patient, they could develop into a cancerous tumour as they continue to grow. Unless new ways are found to induce the cells, the first patients who receive these cells may go on to develop cancer later in life.

summary

▶ Embryos that were created during fertility treatment but are no longer required, are a source of stem cells.

▶ Stem cells can also be taken from embryos that have been created specifically to harvest these cells.

▶ Less versatile stem cells can be found in umbilical cord blood and the placenta, aborted foetuses and in adults.

▶ Scientific techniques are being used to discover new ways of turning adult cells into versatile stem cells.

CHAPTER 3

The ethical issues

Once you start studying living organisms, you run into complicated areas of decision making where people hold different views and come to different conclusions. In studying and using stem cells in science and medicine, there are many areas of concern. To begin with, most stem cells come from embryos, so it is important to consider the status of a human embryo. Religious groups, for example, are often opposed to stem cell research as they consider the destruction of a human embryo as killing a 'life', and this is ethically unacceptable.

Furthermore, before doctors start using an experimental therapy, they need to think about how much risk they should let patients take with their lives if they are offered the chance to be in the first trial group. Another consideration is the role and rights of animals used in medical research, as many of the stem cell research programmes use and kill thousands of mice and other animals every year.

Thinking tools

Over the years philosophers and ethicists have developed many different 'thinking tools' to help us make moral decisions. One method is to aim for the maximum good for the maximum number of people. This is called Utilitarianism. Using this idea you could argue that it is ethically acceptable to damage one embryo, if it leads to a therapy that saves many hundreds of children and adults. Utilitarianism judges whether to do something by looking at the consequences of a procedure and is less concerned about the particular actions involved.

Rules and principles

From another direction of thinking, other people argue that we should lay down some absolute guidelines – some basic rules that cannot be broken. For some

Jeremy Bentham (1748–1832) ▶ was an English philosopher, jurist, and political theorist. He was well-known for advocating Utilitarianism and supported animal rights.

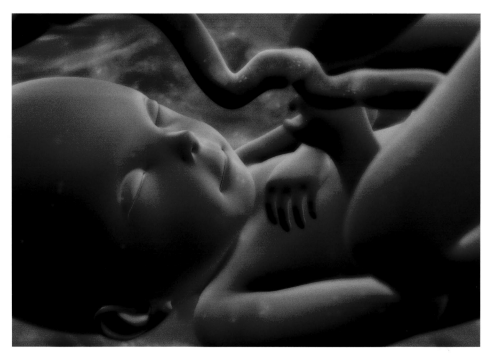

▲ A growing foetus. The rights of a human embryo is one of the main ethical issues regarding stem cell research. The debate often centres around the point at which human life is said to have begun.

people, one rule is that you should never deliberately harm another person, even if you think it will lead to good in the end. This is often combined with a belief that an individual's life starts when a sperm combines with an egg at fertilization to form the first cell of an embryo. Doing anything to damage this embryo would be the same as damaging any other person.

Many doctors around the world use a set of criteria to help with their thinking. Termed Principalism, this approach weighs up four key issues, or principles. The first principle, called autonomy, looks to maximize the way that any donors or recipients are consulted about any risks and benefits, and then encourages these people to take an active role in the decision-making. The second, beneficence, asks that doctors try to maximize benefit to everyone involved. The third principle,

non-maleficence, asks that they do all that is possible to avoid unnecessary harm. And the fourth principle, justice, says that resources should be shared in the best possible way.

viewpoints

'We would pay a price of working on some human embryos, but the benefit would come back in treatment of society itself. Accept there is a cost and get on with it in a carefully regulated context.'
Brian Chapman, Parkinson's disease patient

'We can't ever find something that can counterbalance the direct killing of a life, and when we destroy an embryo to get embryonic stem cells, that is what we do. That is an absolute. We must protect all life.'
John Deighan, Catholic Church Parliamentary Officer, Scotland

Status of an embryo

Much of the controversy surrounding stems cells rests on different people's understanding of the status of an embryo. Is the embryo simply a ball of human cells, or does it have more significance? Is it an independent life in the same way that a breathing and thinking baby is? Should we consider it to have the same value as a child or an adult? Principalism (see page 19) asks for the consideration of how the autonomy of each person is affected by a procedure. So do scientists need to consider the embryo's autonomy?

Some people argue that if the embryo is simply a ball of cells, then it should treated as just that. After all, no one worries about the cells scraped off in a graze, or the blood cells that stick to plaster. Most people agree that embryos are different, because, if given the right conditions and placed in a womb, they can grow into full babies. Does this mean their status is significant enough for their rights to be protected?

The HFE Act

In 1994 the UK government brought in a new law. Called the Human Fertilization and Embryology Act, this document set out guidelines drawn on a particular way of thinking. The basic argument starts by recognising that a dead human body is not considered a person, because it is recognised that that person has died. Current thinking says that a person is counted as having died once their brain has ceased to function. Doctors say the person is 'brain dead'. Once a person is brain dead, most people believe that it is

▲ The UK Parliament was one of the first legislative bodies to consider the implications of scientific research on embryos.

case study

The beginning of legislation

The UK Human Fertilization and Embryology Act of 1994 was the world's first legislation that attempted to create boundaries in the way that scientists could use embryos. The act said that human embryos should be given considerable respect, but could still be used in research if all of the following points were met:

- There was no alternative.

- There was a significant medical goal.

- The embryo was less than 14 days old.

- The research was carefully regulated.

ethically acceptable to remove the organs and transplant them into another person. This is what happens in a kidney, lung or heart transplant.

The next step in the argument is to say that if people are dead once their brains have stopped working, it is not possible to say that they are alive before their brains have started to work. If an embryo is less than 14 days old, it has no nerve cells, so it has no brain. The final step says that as an embryo under 14 days has no brain, it cannot be a living person. In this case, it is ethically possible to use its cells, just as organs are used in organ donation.

This line of thinking led to the HFE Act saying that it was acceptable to experiment on human embryos, as long as they were less than 14 days old. Stem cell scientists carry out research using embryos that are around five to six days old.

It's a fact

In a human embryo, the very first stages of the nervous system and the brain begin to develop once it is about 17 days old.

▲ Baroness Mary Warnock has been at the centre of debate about the ethical status of human embryos. Between 1982 and 1984 she led a major UK Parliamentary enquiry into human fertilization and embryology. The findings of this enquiry formed the basis for the UK's HFE Act.

Religious views

Many people's ethical thinking and decision-making is often guided by their religious or spiritual belief. Most world religions teach that all human life is sacred and have a view on whether or not, or at what point, an embryo is considered a human being. It is these views which often shape ethical beliefs about stem cell research.

Christian views

As is the case with most ethical issues, Christians hold a range of views about the status of human embryos. All Christians agree that a person's life is a gift from God. For some Christian groups, such as the Roman Catholic Church, an embryo should be given full human status the moment that an egg and sperm combine.

Christians who believe that full status starts at fertilization, point to verses in the Old Testament that talk of God watching, caring for and nurturing a person as they grow in the womb. In Psalm 139 verse 16 it says 'your eyes saw my unformed body.' The Psalm goes on to say that God knits us together, and that God has a never-ending relationship with us. The idea that God cares about us as we grow in the womb indicates that Christianity teaches that all humans should show the same care. They say that there is no clear point between fertilization and birth when there is a sudden change in the embryo, and argue that the only clear change happens at fertilization. Therefore, we must treat the embryo as a full human with full human rights from the moment sperm and egg combine.

Other Christian groups say that life is about human relationships, and this starts when the embryo becomes implanted in the mother's womb. This occurs when the embryo is about 10 days old. They say that this creates a step change in the embryo's status. This means that these Christians may permit some use of embryos that have not implanted. The Methodist Church, for example, says it is acceptable to use spare embryonic cells from IVF. However, it is opposed to the

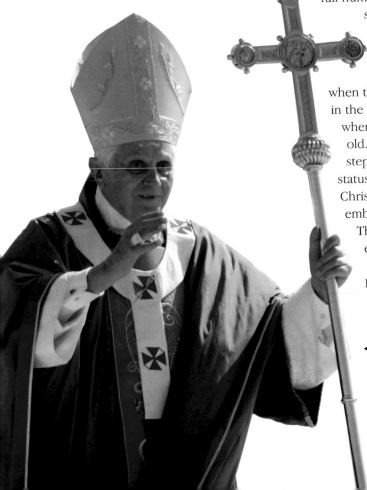

◀ As head of the Roman Catholic Church, Pope Benedict XVI firmly believes that embryos have full human status from the time the egg is fertilized by a sperm.

▲ While Jewish scripture places a high value on human life, the religion does agree that there are benefits to be drawn from stem cell research.

creation of embryos just to be used in research or medical treatments.

Jewish views

Judaism affirms that human life is sacred and must be protected and respected. The religion teaches that human life is a gift from God and that we are its trustees rather than its owners. Judaism accepts both embryonic and adult stem cell research for medical or therapeutic purposes only. As a result, embryos that come from fertility treatment can be used to create stem cells if this will improve our general understanding or cure illness.

Islamic views

In Islam, which has no official position on stem cell research, a key issue is the moment when a person's soul enters an embryo. Before this 'ensoulment' the embryo is not seen as a completely formed human and so most Islamic schools of law would say that it can be used in medical research. However, there is a debate within the Islamic community about exactly when the soul enters an embryo, with some Muslims believing it occurs as early as 40 days after fertilization and others saying it is as late as 120 days.

In the case of human embryonic stem cell research, the Islamic views about 'ensoulment' mean that most would say that it is ethically permissible to allow stem cell research up to 40 days after fertilization. However some Muslims argue that the destruction of an embryo at any stage is ethically unacceptable.

Hindu views

Hinduism teaches that the divine resides in every living thing. Hindus believes all life, no matter in what form, needs to be defended and any act of violence against a living entity is an act of violence against the divine. So, while Hindusim has no official stance on stem cell research, as the human embryo is considered a life from fertilization, the religion would agree that embryos should not be used as a source of stem cells.

Sikh views

Sikhism has no official position on stem cell research but does teach that all human actions should be guided by the belief that the world was divinely created. As such, many Sikhs would agree that the use of human embryos in stem cell research is ethically unacceptable. However, most Sikhs would want to weigh the possibility of developing cures for life-threatening illnesses against the destruction of human embryos for medical research purposes.

Buddhist views

There is no official Buddhist viewpoint on human embryonic stem cell research.

◄ As an embryo is a living thing, and the divine exists in every living thing, most Hindus would not want it to be destroyed for stem cell research purposes.

Buddhism teaches that if a being can sense its surroundings and can feel pain and suffering, whether human or animal, it is considered a 'sentient' being, and so should be protected. Some buddhists may believe working on early embryos is acceptable as these embryos do not yet have nerves and so cannot feel pain or suffering. Others would argue that the destruction of embryos goes against the Buddhist principle of not harming or destroying others.

Followers of Buddhism would want to consider the long-term benefit or harm that could come from stem cell research, as well as the motivation that leads people to use human embryonic stem cells. If people are using human embryos with a genuine desire to heal people, then this is more acceptable and is in accord with the Buddhist principle of pursuing knowledge to help others.

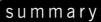

summary

▶ The HFE Act was one of the world's first attempts at regulating the use of embryos for scientific purposes.

▶ When facing ethical dilemmas some people use four basic principles to help them make decisions.

▶ Utilitarians believe something is ethical if it gives greater benefits to people, even though it may also cause some harm.

▶ Christianity says that the human embryo has a high status and should be treated with dignity. While some Christian groups say that this means embryos can be used in certain types of stem cell research, others argue that any use of human embryos is ethically unacceptable.

▶ The Jewish faith teaches that all life is a gift from God and should be respected.

▶ Some Muslims believe that it is acceptable to use early embryos as a source of stem cell research.

▶ Hindusim and Buddhism have no official position on the use of embryos in research.

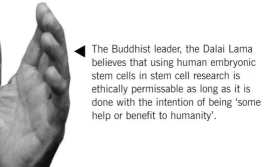

◀ The Buddhist leader, the Dalai Lama believes that using human embryonic stem cells in stem cell research is ethically permissible as long as it is done with the intention of being 'some help or benefit to humanity'.

CHAPTER 4

The possibilities of stem cell research

To date the most frequent medical use of stem cells has been in bone marrow transplants. Bone marrow is vital to life. Packed into the centre of the long bones in our arms and legs, as well as the large bones of our pelvis, bone marrow builds blood cells. Each day millions of blood cells die and are dismantled. The supply of blood cells in the body is kept constant because the bone marrow builds more.

This is possible because the marrow contains somatic stem cells. Day after day the cells grow and divide, each time generating cells that mature into various types of blood cell. The stem cells, however, remain unchanged, ready to generate more and more blood cells throughout the person's life.

Treating leukemia

Occasionally some of the cells start to behave abnormally. In a disease called leukemia, they produce very large numbers of certain types of blood cells which do not function properly. Between the 1950s and 1970s a team at the Fred Hutchinson Cancer Research Center in Seattle, US, showed that it was possible to take bone marrow stem cells from one animal, purify them and inject them into another animal's blood stream. These new cells then moved into the new animal's bone marrow. The leader of this research project, E. Donnall Thomas, won the Nobel Prize in Physiology or Medicine in 1990 for this breakthrough.

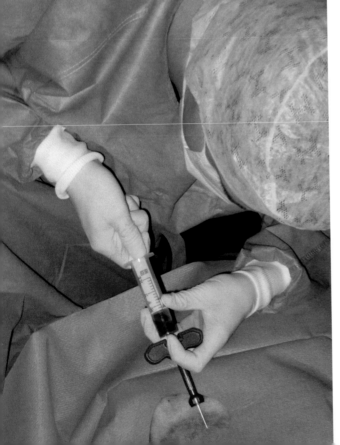

◀ Taking bone marrow from a donor needs to be done with great care. The stem cells that are collected may be able to save someone else's life.

While this scientific research did not use human embryonic stem cells, it raised other ethical issues, such as the use of animals in scientific research, as well as concerns over the long-term effects of the treatment upon the patient.

However, over time this research project developed into a treatment for leukemia. First doctors give the patient chemicals that kill off all of their damaged bone marrow. They then inject healthy bone marrow stem cells that have been collected from a donor into the patient's blood stream. In the human population there are many cell variations, and it is essential that the donated cells match the patient's own cells. If they do not, the patient's body will kill off the new cells. If they match, these new cells travel to the centre of the bones and set up new populations of stem cells. These new stem cells go on to produce healthy red blood cells and this often means the patient is cured.

It's a fact

Each red blood cell only lives for about 120 days. To keep a constant supply, the body needs to make around three million red blood cells a second, which means a healthy body produces about 260,000 million each day.

case study

Pioneering research

In 1959 French cancer specialist Dr Georges Mathé became the first person to inject bone marrow into humans, when he placed stem cells into four Yugoslavian nuclear workers. The workers were suffering because the radiation in their work place had damaged their own bone marrow so that it could no longer manufacture blood cells properly. A few years later Mathé developed a way of using bone marrow transplants to treat people whose bone marrow had been damaged by leukemia, a type of cancer that stops bone marrow working properly. In both research cases all of the patients were healed.

◄ Dr Georges Mathé died in 2010, but his research led to thousands of lives being saved.

Searching for a match

Transplant operations such as bone marrow transplants work well, but only if the stem cells that are given to the patient come from someone who has what doctors call a very similar 'tissue type'. Our cells are coated in markers. It is as if they are wearing security badges. White blood cells patrol the body, checking that all the cells have these markers. If they find a cell with a strange marker, such as a different tissue type, they presume that it has invaded the body and destroy it. By doing this the white cells get rid of invading bacteria, but can also damage cells that may have been injected to try and cure disease.

Some people have a rare tissue type, and doctors have great difficulty finding suitable donors. The most likely donors are close relatives, especially brothers and sisters. One question then is, should someone be compelled to be tested and give a donation if their blood cells could save another person's life? Giving bone marrow is a painful procedure, and all medical procedures carry some risk. A donor may feel more willing to give bone marrow to save their sibling, but less willing if they have never met the patient.

A few parents of ill children have chosen to have more children in the hope that a new child will be a good match. If so, scientists may be able to take stem cells from the new baby's umbilical cord blood to treat the ill sibling and potentially save his or her life.

▼ In the film *My Sister's Keeper*, based on the fictional book of the same title, the character of Anna (right) was born to try and save her sister Kate's life (left). The book and film raised ethical questions about Anna's right to choose what medical procedures she underwent in order to save her sister.

Created to save a life

In the future scientists may be able to create embryos using sperm and eggs from a patient's parents, and then test the embryos to see if any are a good match. If any are a match, the embryo could be turned into stem cells and used to cure the patient. There are problems and risks however. This procedure would take months to test and find an embryo with a similar tissue type, and then there would be a nine-month wait for the baby to be born. There is the risk that the patient will not survive long enough. In addition, many people find it ethically unacceptable to create embryos 'to order'. Furthermore, scientists may have to create more than one embryo to find one with the right tissue type. Parents may then have to decide what to do with the other embryos – use them in research, have further children or destroy them?

case study

To save a sibling

Lisa and Jack Nash's first child, Molly, was born with Fanconi anaemia, a genetic disorder that prevented her bone marrow from working properly. She needed a transplant of life-giving stem cells, but doctors could not find anyone with a matching tissue type. Doctors used Lisa and Jack's eggs and sperm, and created many embryos. They tested individual cells from the embryos to find one that matched Molly's tissues and was free from the genetic disease. This embryo was implanted in Lisa's womb.

Nine months later, in August 2000, Adam was born in a Chicago hospital. Cells from his umbilical cord saved his sister's life. Lisa Nash said, 'we wanted a child who would not suffer the way Molly suffered. And we made a decision for our family, not for the world to take issue.'

▲ Using a specifically created embryo let doctors successfully treat Lisa and Jack's daughter. Doctors used the stem cells from her brother Adam's umbilical cord to boost Molly's own immune system.

Other organs

While organs like bone marrow, blood and the liver are very good at rebuilding themselves, others are much less able. The body has difficulty restoring organs like the heart, brain and the nervous system if they are damaged.

In a heart attack, for instance, blood stops flowing to some or all parts of the heart muscle. These areas of muscle run out of oxygen and build up waste products that would normally have been removed. Consequently, cells in the area stop working properly or die and that area of the heart that can never work again. The same happens in the brain where disease or injury can damage areas of nervous tissue. The reason is that each of these organs has few, if any, stem cells and cannot generate replacement healthy cells.

First time treatment risks

There are benefits to be drawn from stem cell research and consquently stem cell treatment. In one experiment, scientists have taken somatic stem cells and treated them so that they start to produce heart muscle cells. They have then been able to inject these cells into a damaged heart and restore some of the heart's function. Yet there are risks involved, as once the cells are put in, they cannot be taken out. While scientists have watched what happens to these sorts of cells over the first few months after they have been injected into animals in laboratory conditions, no one yet knows how the cells will behave over a few years or in humans. There is a risk that they could cause damage, or even trigger cancerous tumours to develop. So the first patients who try this new treatment are taking a considerable risk.

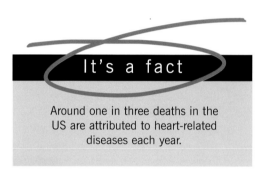

It's a fact

Around one in three deaths in the US are attributed to heart-related diseases each year.

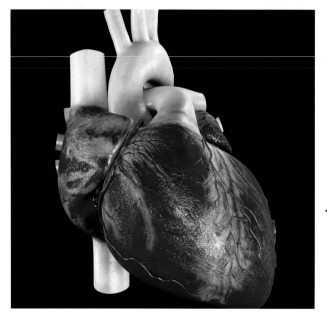

◀ Scientists in Holland have managed to grow cardiac muscle stem cells from adult human hearts, rather than human embryonic stem cells. This removes the ethical issue of using human embryos in some stem cell research.

Some people believe that patients who are already ill should not be exposed to more risk. Other people believe that patients who would die without a new treatment should be allowed to take the risk if they wish to, as it may prolong their life.

case study

Building a new piece of trachea

In 2008, when Columbian mother of two Claudia Castillo caught tuberculosis, the disease severely damaged her trachea, the pipe that lets air flow into her lungs. The only solution normally available is to remove the damaged tube and remove the lung. This would have been a huge and dangerous operation.

Instead, a team of scientists and doctors working in Bristol, Barcelona, Milan and Padua took a 15 centimetre-long section of trachea from the body of a 51-year-old man who had died of a stroke. They spent the next six weeks removing all of the cells and leaving just the cartilage frame. While they were doing this, doctors took a sample of bone marrow cells from 30-year-old Claudia, isolated the stem cells and grew them carefully in a laboratory. Once the donated trachea was free of its original cells, they coated it with Claudia's stem cells. These stem cells grew and rebuilt the section of trachea, which surgeons then used to cure the patient.

While many people are worried about the ethical acceptability of stem cell therapies that involve embryos, this treatment had no such ethical problems because it used the patient's own cells.

▼ Building a new section of trachea (below) for Claudia has meant that doctors have been able to move into an exciting new area of medicine and stem cell research.

Testing on animals

It is not easy to cure diseases. First scientists must understand what goes wrong when a disease strikes, and then look to develop ways of stopping this occurring. In a disease like cancer, for instance, scientists need to understand what happens in a cell that causes it to keep on growing and dividing. They then need to find ways of preventing this. While stem cells are playing an important role in this research, a lot of the research involves testing on animals. This raises ethical issues over the use and treatment of animals for research purposes.

Over recent years, scientists have bred a strain of mice known as nude mice. The first thing you notice when you look at them is that they have no hair. What is less obvious is that these mice do not tend to reject cells that are injected into them. This means that scientists can inject stem cells that have been specially chosen because they will create specific types of cancerous tumour. The mice then develop that type of cancer. As the cancer grows, the scientist can study the tumour to learn more about it. They can also give the mouse different potential anti-cancer treatments to see which are most effective. This type of research has increased our understanding of cancer, but it also uses, and kills, thousands of mice each year.

Testing with stem cells alone

Scientists have another way of using stem cells in the laboratory that avoids using animals. In one set of experiments, scientists have studied how to treat people with a disease called spinal muscular atrophy.

▼ Scientists have deliberately bred these mice so that their immune system doesn't work properly. They can be used to test new ideas involving stem cells. However, the use of animals in medical research raises other ethical issues.

▲ Animal rights activists protest against animal research at the University of California, Los Angeles, 22 April, 2009.

These people have an error in the genetic instructions inside their cells, and the error causes nerves that send signals to their muscles to stop working. As a result, the patient becomes weak and eventually paralysed. Scientists collected skin cells from these patients, and inserted a virus into the cells. This virus turned the cells into stem cells carrying the disease. This meant scientists could grow a population of cells that all have this same genetic error. They could then inject thousands of different chemicals in to the cells to see if any kept the cells healthy. Scientists can then use these findings to form a new therapy for spinal muscular atrophy.

viewpoints

'I abhor vivisection with my whole soul. All the scientific discoveries stained with innocent blood I count as of no consequence.'
Mahatma Gandhi

'[Genetically altered mice] truly provided a revolution in mammalian biology... It is not an exaggeration to say that there is no mammalian biologist today who does not use these tools in one way or another.'
Raju Kucherlapti, a Harvard University geneticist,1988

It's a fact

According to the Home Office, 414,287 mice were used in medical experiments in the UK in 2009.

Safety and autonomous choice

In November 2010, doctors working in Scotland started the first clinical trial that involved injecting stem cells into the brains of people who had suffered a type of stroke. In these patients, a blood clot had formed somewhere in the body and then travelled along a blood vessel into the brain. It had blocked the vessel so that no blood could flow to a part of the brain. As a result, the nerve cells in that area of the brain had stopped working.

To treat this, doctors injected human embryonic stem cells into the damaged area of the brain. The first trials did not aim to heal the person, but to check that the stem cells caused no harm. To do this, they only injected a few cells – two million. This may seem a lot, but scientists would probably need to inject more like 100 million cells if they hoped to cure someone. The doctors will now monitor this person for the next two years to see what happens. If all goes well, they will go on to give higher doses to other patients.

Being the first patient is always risky. Although new treatments can be tested on laboratory animals, no one knows what will happen in humans until the treatment is tested on patients. Patients want to live for many years after treatment, and there is no way of testing the treatment's long term effects or safety on animals, as the result may differ in humans. However, people argue that the patients are not forced to be involved; they are exercising their own autonomous choice. Other people feel the treatment is ethically

▼ Studying brain scans gives doctors a way of assessing the damage caused by a stroke. The scans can also be used to show if new stem cell therapies are working.

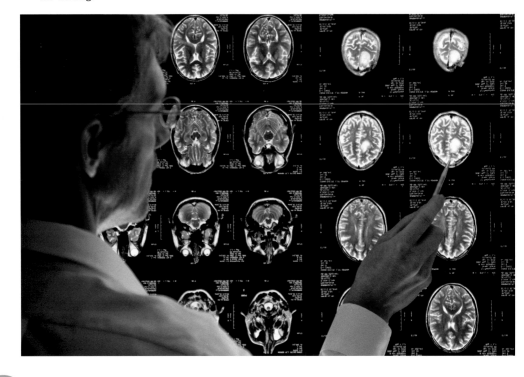

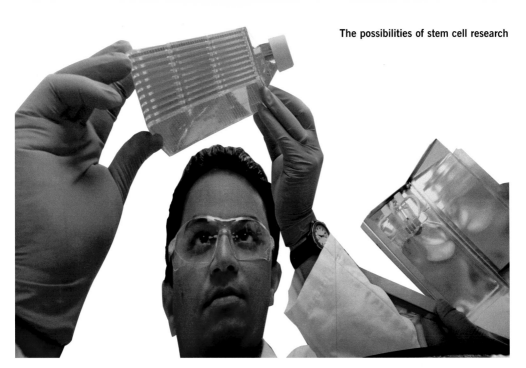

▲ An exhibit at the 2010 World Stem Cell Summit. More than 1,200 scientists from around the world attended the summit, which focuses on the advancement of embryonic stem cell research.

unacceptable because the stem cells used in this trial experiment originally came from an aborted human foetus. While the abortion was carried out legally, some people say that the foetus was never given any choice.

viewpoints

'I am pro-life. I believe human life begins at conception. I also believe that embryonic stem cell research should be encouraged and supported.'
Bill Frist, US physician and politician, 29 July, 2005

'The best that can be said about embryonic stem cell research is that it is scientific exploration into the potential benefits of killing human beings.'
Tom DeLay, *Washington Post*, 25 May, 2005

summary

▶ For 50 years, doctors have transplanted stem cells into bone marrow to cure people with luekemia.

▶ Taking stem cells from adult donors has fewer ethical problems than taking them from embryos.

▶ Some people think that treatments involving stem cells taken from embryos or aborted foetuses are unethical.

▶ Creating a new embryo or baby to donate cells is one way of providing perfectly matching stem cells, but some people worry that the new baby is being treated as a commodity and not as a person.

▶ The first patients to receive a new stem cell therapy take a risk that the cells could do more harm than good, but it is their choice to take part in the trial.

CHAPTER 5

Legal rulings on stem cell use

Scientific and medical developments might start in laboratories, but they soon affect many different people. For that reason, governments around the world often set up laws that say what sort of research can and cannot be done. Many countries have rules about the way that animals must be treated when they are used in research, and an increasing number of countries have laws that set boundaries around research involving stem cells.

The public funds debate in the US

Soon after scientists started to see ways of using stem cells from foetuses and embryos, public opinion was divided. In 1974 the members of the 93rd US Congress decided to ban any government funded work that used stem cells from foetuses and embryos until they were able to fully assess the issues. Over the following decades successive Presidents have lifted the ban, and then re-imposed new bans numerous times. Each time the decision has rested on whether an embryo should have the same human rights as a baby, child or adult.

In the US the debate focused on whether it was right to use public money to fund

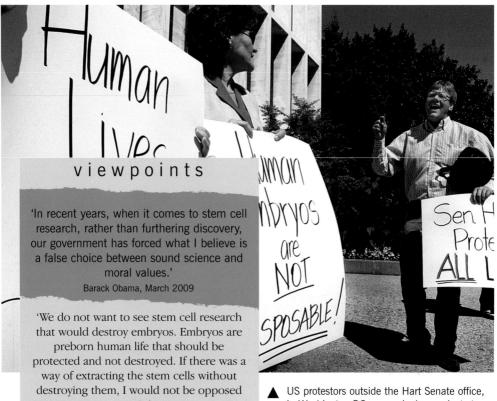

viewpoints

'In recent years, when it comes to stem cell research, rather than furthering discovery, our government has forced what I believe is a false choice between sound science and moral values.'
Barack Obama, March 2009

'We do not want to see stem cell research that would destroy embryos. Embryos are preborn human life that should be protected and not destroyed. If there was a way of extracting the stem cells without destroying them, I would not be opposed to it.'
Ron Stoddard, executive director of
Nightlight Christian Adoptions, August 2010

▲ US protestors outside the Hart Senate office, in Washington DC, campaigning against stem cell research.

research. There is a strong view in the US that people should have a lot of freedom with how they spend their own money, so many private companies have been involved in funding stem cell research. As a result, some private companies took embryos and used them to create stem cells. If looked after, these stem cells will continue growing indefinitely. Many scientists then suggested that even if you did not approve of the way these cells came into existence, it would be wrong not to use them as it would mean that an embryo had been destroyed, but nothing had been gained in return. The stem cells would be wasted if the embryos were simply destroyed. Even so, some people think that it is still unethical to use these cells. Furthermore, the involvement of profit-making businesses in stem cell research raises more ethical issues, with some people arguing that private companies may be tempted to ignore ethical issues as they seek profits.

In 2001, President George W. Bush decided that any human embryonic stem cells created up until that year could be used in publically funded research, but no new ones could be generated. However, just after coming to power in 2009, President Obama signed an executive order overturning that ban. Now, public money can be used to fund many forms of research that uses human embryos.

▼ In 2009 President Obama signed an executive order reversing stem cell research restrictions that were put in place in 2001 by President Bush.

Varying views around Europe

Within Europe there is a wide range of views about the ways that stem cells should be used. Once again, most of the disagreements rest on different countries' views about the ethical status of human embryos.

The UK's Human Fertilization and Embryology Act (see page 20) was one of the first pieces of legislation that tried to establish boundaries for ethical research on human embryos. As this Act allows for research on embryos before they are 14 days old, scientists in the UK are then free to use and create human embryos as sources of stem cells. The work is regulated and has to be carried out under careful supervision, but it can go ahead. This means that scientific research can continue but lets the public know that there are clear ethical guidelines around the work.

In Germany and Italy, scientists are not allowed to deliberately create embryos, but they can import embryos that have been created in other countries. Denmark only allows embryos to be used in stem cell research if they are 'spare' embryos from fertility clinics. Their argument is that the embryos already exist and are unwanted, and throwing them away would be more unethical than using them.

▼ In 1997 the European Parliament in Strasbourg drew up a convention protecting human rights, including the use of embryos in scientific research. It is then up to each nation's government to decide which bits of the convention they want to adopt as part of their own country's laws.

▼ Article 18 of the European Convention on Human Rights and Biomedicine (1997) states that 'the creation of human embryos for research purposes is prohibited.' By 2011 more than half of the 47 European countries had adopted this convention into their own nation's laws.

27 countries have signed and enforced the convention on embryo use		20 countries have not made the convention part of their national laws
Bosnia and Herzegovina	Bulgaria	Albania
Croatia	Cyprus	Andorra
Czech Republic	Denmark	Armenia
Estonia	Finland	Austria
Georgia	Greece	Azerbaijan
Hungary	Iceland	France
Latvia	Lithuania	Germany
Malta	Moldova	Ireland
Montenegro	Norway	Italy
Portugal	Romania	Lichtenstein
San Marino	Slovakia	Luxembourg
Slovenia	Spain	Malta
Switzerland	The former Yugoslav	Monaco
Turkey	Republic of Macedonia	Netherlands
		Poland
		Russia
		Serbia
		Sweden
		Ukraine
		United Kingdom

viewpoints

'The UK should spend at least an additional £350 million over the next decade on stem cell research if we wish to maintain our international leadership in this area. It is vital that we maintain and increase the level of public funding. The ultimate health and wealth gains the UK will enjoy are directly proportional to the additional investment we are proposing.'

Sir John Pattison, chair of the UK Stem Cell Initiative Panel, 2005

'There are two fallacies, one that cures from embryonic stem cells are imminent and the other that adult stem cells are unlikely to be as effective.'

Professor Neil Scolding, Frenchay Hospital, Bristol, UK, 2001

The rest of the world

Many countries around the world have no laws or regulations about what scientists can or cannot do with human embryos and stem cells. For example China, Argentina and Iceland all have no legislation in this area. This effectively means that there are no limits to the sort of work that can be carried out in these countries.

Some scientists think that this gives people working in these countries an unfair advantage, and that scientists working there will be able to race ahead of everywhere else. Other people argue that scientists perform more careful research when they are in areas that have restrictions, and that this work has a greater chance of getting usable results.

In the last decade, China has worked hard to build its capacity for research in many areas, including looking to see how scientists can use stem cells to treat people. The government has actively encouraged Chinese scientists to be trained abroad and then return to work in China. It has also provided lots of money to carry out this research. The Chinese government has kept regulations as light as possible and has a goal of moving rapidly from discovering possibilities to testing out this research on humans. In 2000, Chinese scientists published just 37 scientific reports on stem cells. In 2007, they published 1,116 reports. This is still a long way behind the 6,008 papers published by American stem cell scientists that year,

▼ A patient receiving treatment at the Tiantan Puhua Hospital in Beijing, China, in 2007. Doctors at Tiantan Puhua attempt to treat people with conditions such as stroke and spinal cord injuries by injecting stem cells.

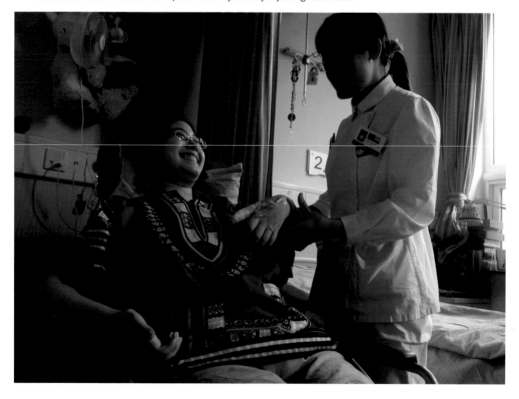

case study

The race for discovery

In February 2004 Korea was pushed to the forefront of the debate on human cloning and stem cells when its scientists announced that they had created cloned human embryos and had produced human embryonic stem cells from a cloned embryo.

Korean scientist Hwang Woo-suk was a national hero when he first told the world about his stem cell research. However, he found himself at the centre of a storm of protest when international scientists discovered he had lied about some of the stem cells in his laboratory and fabricated results published in two world-leading journals. It is possible that this occurred because there is little regulation of research carried out in Korea.

▲ By leading the world in the race to make and control stem cells and their uses, Hwang Woo-suk became a national hero. Internationally, many scientists have expressed concern about his research practices.

but it is similar to the numbers published in the UK, Japan and Germany.

The drawback of light regulation in China is that more than 200 hospitals offer some form of stem cell therapy, but few, if any, of these therapies have been shown to be safe and effective. Some of these therapies encourage foreign visitors to come for treatment. The patients who come are normally desperate to recover from a serious disease but, by taking expensive and unproven treatments, they may risk losing lots of money and being damaged by the treatment.

summary

▶ As a general principle, if a country does not ban something, then it is legal to do it in that country.

▶ Different countries allow different uses of human embryos and stem cells that come from human embryos.

▶ Some countries actively encourage research so that they can boost their economy.

▶ Some countries are more concerned than others about the protection of human embryos.

CHAPTER 6

What does the future hold?

Discovering scientific insights into how cells work, what goes wrong with cells in different diseases and developing new therapies that aim to restore health is costly. It costs hundreds of millions of dollars to have any hope of making progress. On top of this, there is always the risk that any individual piece of research will produce no useful answers.

How then can we afford to fund this work?

Companies exist to make money by selling items or services. Companies are used to the idea of investing at the beginning of a project, but need to have a reasonable chance of earning enough within a few years to pay back the investment and then make a profit. In an area like stem cell research, the chance of producing a workable therapy is small and the costs are high. This might not make stem cell research a viable business investment for some private companies.

The only way forward is for governments to fund the initial research. Companies can then pick up the bits of the research that work, and turn them into profit making therapies.

◀ Stock markets drive business. They demand that companies make profits and this in turn can put pressure on companies working in complex ethical areas such as stem cell research. This can also raise questions about the ethics of funding medical research.

Some people argue that companies should not make profits when they have not paid for the research and that something which is potentially as important to humanity as stem cell research should not be in the hands of private investors.

Patent your findings

When companies do invest in research, they protect their findings with patents. A patent is a legal document that lets someone tell others about their work, but prevents anyone else from using the information without paying a fee. Patents are supposed to be granted only for inventions. Historically they have not been given to people who have discovered something that already exists. For example, a botanist cannot patent a species of plant just because they were the first person to identify it. Lawyers and scientists argue about whether it should be possible to patent something like a stem cell, because some people think that it is much more of a discovery than an invention.

Where should eggs come from in the future?

Scientists who deliberately create embryos find that their work is slowed down because there is a shortage of human eggs. They want to pay women for their eggs, so that the supply will increase. Furthermore, some scientists believe that creating embryos specifically for research is more ethical than taking spare embryos from fertility clinics because these specially created eggs were never intended to develop into a baby. They are only there to provide cells. The opponents disagree saying that this is even worse than creating life through IVF. They argue that scientists are creating new embryos purely to serve a commercial or medical need. They also point out that supplying eggs is a dangerous and painful procedure for any woman, and that paying people to do it means that more women who need money may be encouraged to risk their health or even their life and potentially damage their fertility.

viewpoints

'With a private company, your ethical dilemma is about money: who stands to benefit from this new technology? In federally funded research, your reputation depends on getting 'good' results... If you don't get those results, you're going to have a hard time getting funded.'
Dr Fessler, neurosurgeon, Northwestern Memorial Hospital, Chicago, US

'Some people worry about the ethics of a profit motive in developing health-care mechanisms. I don't happen to agree. The United States has been strong in the field of biomedical enterprise because companies are responding to a marketplace.'
Dr John Cunningham, director of hematopoietic stem cell transplantation, Chicago, US

▲ In 2010, 28-year-old Marje Khan narrowly avoided prosecution when she advertised her eggs for sale in the UK. Under UK law it is illegal to sell human eggs, even if they are your own.

Future, fears and fortunes

So far scientists have learned a remarkably large amount about stem cells in very few years. The ability to use these cells to model disease in laboratory cells and animals has given many new and valuable insights into treatments and cures for diseases. The ability to test new therapies and potential drugs on stem cells that mimic different diseases means that medical research has the opportunity to develop quickly.

There is the possibility of creating tissue grafts for burns patients, stimulating people's cells so that they can grow new teeth where old ones have been lost through injury or decay and repairing nerves that have been damaged by accidents or disease. Some even claim that stem cell therapy could lead to us all living longer as stem cell science lets us rebuild specific bits of our bodies. But no one is suggesting that it will be quick to make these things happen, and many uncertainties still exist. If the ethical and financial problems are not solved, then all the work could lead to nothing.

Supply and justice

In the meantime, critics of stem cell research argue that as interest in stem cells increases, scientists will need more human embryos. This use of embryos may then increase once a treatment is developed, and production will move from laboratories to large factory-based production lines.

If stem cells do provide new treatments, the challenge will be to ensure everyone benefits. It is easy for rich people to use new technologies, but it is not always easy for poor people to get the same access. One ethical principle that policy makers will need to consider is that of justice – how can we make sure that everyone has access to a fair share of treatments?

▼ While stem cells are only used in laboratories, the numbers involved will be relatively small. Numbers will rapidly increase if industrial scale use starts and this may raise more ethical issues.

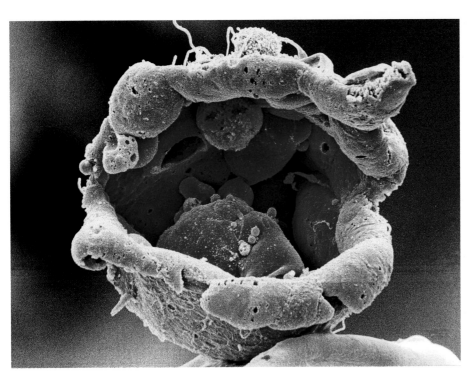

▲ The red coloured stem cells in the middle of this human blastocyst could be used in stem cell research. However, the arguments surrounding this research mean that the ethical dilemma of whether or not human embryonic stem cell use is ethically acceptable remains a much debated issue.

viewpoints

'Researchers and biotech executives foresee the day when the effects of many catastrophic diseases can be reversed. The damaged brains of Alzheimer's disease patients may be restored. Severed spinal cords may be rejoined. Damaged organs may be rebuilt. Stem cells provide hope that this dream will become a reality.'
George Wolff, *The Biotech Investor's Bible*, 2001

'There are perfectly ethical ways of obtaining stem cells to cure disease, which do not involve embryo destruction, so no matter what moral value one places on the human embryo, we do not need to use it.'
Josephine Quintavalle. director of Comment on Reproductive Ethics (CORE), 2004

summary

▶ The research needed to understand and use stem cells will cost vast amounts of money.

▶ Often the goal in privately-funded stem cell research is to make profits for the company, rather than to make advances in medicine.

▶ Pioneering research can only occur if governments fund it.

▶ Companies can then exploit the findings and create therapies that generate profits.

▶ No one expects stem cell therapies to be widely available in the next year or two.

▶ There is a high degree of excitement that over the next decade or two stem cells could transform medicine.

Glossary

Blastocyst A hollow ball of about 250 cells that, in humans, forms around four to six days after fertilization.

Bone marrow The cells that pack the centre of bones, including stem cells that generate new blood cells.

DNA (Deoxyribonucleic Acid) The molecule used to store information inside cells.

Cancer A life-threatening disease caused by cells that will not stop growing.

Cloning The medical process by which the genetic DNA of an individual is identically copied in another embryo.

Embryo The stage of life which, in humans, covers the first eight weeks after fertilization.

Ectoderm The part of an embryo that goes on to form skin, brain, eyes and nervous system.

Embryonic stem cells Stem cells that are taken from the inner cell mass growing inside a blastocyst.

Endoderm The part of an embryo that goes on to form lungs, liver, pancreas and gut lining.

Ensoulment In the Islamic faith, this is the moment when a soul enters a foetus.

Fertilization This process occurs when a sperm meets and breaks into an egg. From now on, the fertilized egg can start to develop into an embryo.

Foetus The stage of development which in humans goes from nine weeks after fertilization until birth.

Gene A section of DNA that gives the instructions needed to build proteins in cells.

Induced pluripotent stem cells Adult cells that have been reprogrammed to have the same adaptability as embryonic stem cells.

In vitro Latin for 'in glass'. This term is commonly used to describe any biological process that scientists and doctors deliberately perform in a laboratory. In vitro fertilization (IVF) is the fertilization of an egg and a sperm in laboratory conditions.

Mesoderm The part of an embryo that goes on to form the skeleton, muscles, blood cells and blood vessels.

Morula A small bundle of cells. The morula forms after fertilization.

Multipotent stem cells Cells capable of forming only a few types of tissue in a mature organism.

Nucleus The part of the cell that contains most of its information, which is stored on chromosomes made of DNA.

Parthenogenesis The ability for an egg to turn into a new individual without being fertilized.

Placenta The organ that forms a link between a mother and her developing baby.

Pluripotent stem cells Cells capable of forming many types of tissue in a mature organism.

Rejection A process whereby the body's defence system destroys cells that look as if they have come from outside the body.

Sibling A brother or sister.

Somatic stem cells Stem cells found in adult organs (and some foetal organs) that give rise to a limited number of cell types. They are sometimes called adult stem cells.

Totipotent stem cells Cells capable of growing into any type of tissue, including those only present during development.

Umbilical cord A cord connecting the foetus to the placenta during pregnancy. It transfers nutrients from the mother to the foetus.

Utilitarianism One approach to ethical thinking that tries to give the maximum benefit to the maximum number of people.

Timeline

1890s First experiments show embryo cells are totipotent.

1908 Russian scientist Alexander Maksimow is the first to use the term 'stem cells'.

1960s Canadian scientists James Till and Ernest McCullock show that bone marrow contains stem cells.

1974 In the US, the 93rd Congress bans most federally funded embryonic tissue research.

1975 Beatrice Mintz and Karl Illmensee at the University of Philadelphia discover that embryonic stem cells can generate organisms.

1978 Stem cells are discovered in human umbilical cords.

1980s First embryonic stem cells extracted from mice.

1981 Both Martin Evans at the University of Cambridge and Gail Martin at the University of California culture pluripotent mouse embryonic stem cells from inner cell masses of blastocysts.

1985-1992 Brigid Hogan at Vanderbilt University of Medicine in Nashville, US, and Peter Donovan at the National Cancer Institute in Maryland, US, make embryonic stem cells turn into specific tissue types.

1988 A California couple conceive a child so scientists can harvest stem cells from the child's umbilical cord blood to treat their 17-year-old daughter.

1993 President Bill Clinton lifts the twenty-year ban on embryonic tissue research.

1994 The UK Parliament passes the Human Fertilization and Embryology Act.

1997 US biologist James Thomson gets stem cell lines from embryos donated by in vitro fertilization clinics.

1997 US scientist John Gearhart gets primordial germ cells from aborted foetuses.

1998 US biologist James Thomson sets up the world's first batch of human embryonic stem cells – they are still growing today.

2001 President George W. Bush imposes restrictions on human embryonic stem cell research in the US.

2005 US scientist Robert Lanza's team establishes embryonic stem cell lines from one cell of an eight-cell mouse embryo, while letting the rest of the embryo develop.

2007 Japanese researcher Shinya Yamanaka and James Thomson both discover how to create induced pluripotent stem cells from skin cells.

2009 President Barack Obama removes many barriers to research involving human stem cells in the US.

2010 Human clinical trials start using human embryonic stem cells.

Further information

Websites:

http://www.internationalstemcell.com/

The first company to deliberately produce stem cells by parthenogenesis.

http://www.ukstemcellbank.org.uk

The website of the UK stem cell bank which manages the storage of human embryonic foetal and somatic stem cells.

http://www.eurostemcell.org/

Downloadable films and resources for use in schools and colleges, that investigate the science, uses and ethics of stem cells.

http://www.garlandscience.com/textbooks/cbl /stemcell/corematerials/timeline.html

An expanded timeline of stem cell research and legal arguments.

http://www.stemcelltracker.com/2009/02/ste m cell-research-breakthroughs.html

A timeline of scientific findings.

Index

Numbers in **bold** refer to illustrations